P9-DMV-164

ULTIMATE CAR BATTLES

JAGUAR vs. ASTON MARTIN

Colin Crum

WINDMILL
BOOKS
New York

Published in 2014 by Windmill Books, An Imprint of Rosen Publishing
29 East 21st Street, New York, NY 10010

First Edition

Produced for Windmill by Cyan Candy, LLC
Designer: Erica Clendening, Cyan Candy
Editor for Windmill: Joshua Shadowens

Photo Credits: Cover (top) EML/Shutterstock.com; cover (bottom), 30 (bottom)
KENCKOphotography/Shutterstock.com; pp. 4, 18, 22 Darren Brode/Shutterstock.com; pp. 5,
14, 20 Max Earey/Shutterstock.com; pp. 6, 11, 25 DDCoral/Shutterstock.com; p. 7 Pan Xunbin/
Shutterstock.com; p. 8 lendy16/Shutterstock.com; p. 9 Radoslaw Lecyk/Shutterstock.com; pp.
10, 12 DeepGreen/Shutterstock.com; p. 13 TanArt/Shutterstock.com; p.15 Fedor Selivanov/
Shutterstock.com; p.16 Vorotylin Roman/Shutterstock.com; p. 17 Roberto Cerruti/Shutterstock.
com; p. 19 Daniel Goodings/Shutterstock.com; p. 21 cjmac/Shutterstock.com; p. 23 Paulo M.
F. Pires/Shutterstock.com; p. 24 Maksim Toome/Shutterstock.com; p. 26 Dongliu/Shutterstock.
com; p. 27 Sam Moores/Shutterstock.com; p. 30 (top) Stefan Ataman/Shutterstock.com.

Library of Congress Cataloging-in-Publication Data

Crum, Colin.
 Jaguar vs. Aston Martin / by Colin Crum. — First edition.
     pages cm. — (Ultimate car battles)
 Includes index.
 ISBN 978-1-4777-9015-1 (library) — ISBN 978-1-4777-9016-8 (pbk.) —
 ISBN 978-1-4777-9017-5 (6-pack)
 1. Jaguar automobile—Juvenile literature. 2. Aston Martin automobile—Juvenile literature. I.
Title. II. Title: Jaguar versus Aston Martin.
 TL215.J3C78 2014

TABLE OF CONTENTS

BATTLE OF THE BRITS

If British sports cars are known for one thing, it is being super cool! For example, James Bond, the coolest spy in movie history, is famous for driving slick British sports cars. Two British carmakers in particular are known for making cool sports cars. These companies are Jaguar and Aston Martin.

Aston Martin and Jaguar have been **rivals** for more than 75 years. Both

2014 Jaguar F-Type

Here, the 2012 Aston Martin V8 Vantage S is shown at the 2011 Geneva Motor Show. This car is built with a 4.7-liter V8 engine and a 7-speed manual transmission.

companies make eye-catching cars known for their speed, beauty, and **luxury** features. The Aston Martin DB5 and the Jaguar E-Type are examples of some of the coolest cars of all time!

Aston Martin cars are much more expensive than Jaguars. Depending on the model, you could buy two Jaguars for the price of one Aston Martin! However, both brands have an **exclusive** image that makes people want to buy their cars.

WHAT MAKES A JAGUAR?

Jaguar is one of the most famous names in luxury sports cars. Jaguar has been making stylish, high-performance cars for more than 75 years! People love to drive them and collect them.

Jaguar is named for a species of big cat. Wild jaguars are known for being fast, powerful, and beautiful, just like the cars! In England, people pronounce Jaguar as "JAG-yoo-ahr." In the United States, most people say, "JA-gwahr."

Jaguar Logo

This is a 2011 Jaguar XKR sports car. This stylish car is built with a powerful supercharged V8 engine. When people think of Jaguar, they think of power and beauty!

Jaguar Cars is a part of Jaguar Land Rover, which is owned by Tata Motors. In the past, Jaguar has been owned by British Leyland and the Ford Motor Company. Today, their headquarters is in Whitley, England.

The Prime Minister's Jaguars

Since 2010, Jaguars have been used as the British Prime Minister's official car. These Jaguars are specially designed XJ Sentinels. They are built with armored cabins and bulletproof glass to keep the Prime Minister safe. They also have many other special features, such as night vision and high-definition televisions.

ALL ABOUT ASTON MARTIN

Many people think of Aston Martins as the ultimate British sports car. For more than 100 years, Aston Martin has been making super fast cars known for their sleek design.

Aston Martin cars are very expensive. The least expensive 2014 Aston Martin is a Cygnet. It costs a little under $40,000. A 2014 Aston Martin Vanquish costs more than $275,000!

Here you can see an Aston Martin DBS, built with a V12 engine. This high-performance model was made between 2007 and 2012. Today, it has been replaced with the V12 Vanquish.

This is a 1959 Aston Martin DB 2/4 Mark III sports car. The car was designed with a new grille shape that is still used on Aston Martin models today!

Aston Martin opened a new headquarters in Gaydon, England in 2003. Today, Aston Martin is owned in part by the Ford Motor Company. However, it is mostly owned by a group of private investors. Aston Martin's logo is a pair of wings.

Celebrating 100 Years

In 2013, Aston Martin had its 100th anniversary. To celebrate, the company designed special **limited edition** versions of the V8 Vantage, DB9, Rapide, and Vanquish models. Just 100 cars were built for each model, and each car was numbered. The paint on the outside of these cars fades from dark silver to light silver.

THE START OF JAGUAR

In 1922, William Lyons and William Walmsley started the Swallow Sidecar Company. They wanted to build motorcycle sidecars. However, by 1927, their company started making automobiles as well.

The first car with the Jaguar name was the 1935 SS Jaguar 2.5 Litre Saloon. In 1936, the Jaguar SS100 became the first Jaguar sports car sold. It had a top speed of more than 100 miles per hour (161 km/h).

1937 Jaguar
SS100

The SS100 could go from 0 to 60 miles per hour (0–97 km/h) in 13.5 seconds. Here, you can see a vintage red SS100 at a car show.

However, the SS100 was known for giving drivers a bumpy ride! By 1945, Lyons changed the company's name to Jaguar Cars.

The next Jaguar sports car was the XK120. Jaguar introduced this roadster at the 1948 London Motor Show. At the time, it was the fastest road car in **production**! The XK120 was built with Jaguar's new XK engine and could reach 120 miles per hour (193 km/h).

ASTON MARTIN'S BEGINNINGS

Aston Martin got its start in 1913. Lionel Martin founded the company with his friend Robert Bamford. After winning the Aston Hill Climb car race, Martin wanted to build his own cars. The first Aston Martin car was built in 1915 in Kensington, England. By 1922, Aston Martin was making cars to race in the French Grand Prix.

Aston Martin had a lot of money troubles in the 1920s and 1930s. They built road cars and racecars, including the T-Type, International,

1952 Aston Martin DB2 Coupe

Here you can see one of Aston Martin's early racecars, the Aston Martin Ulster. An Ulster came in third place at the 1935 24 Hours of Le Mans race.

Le Mans, and MKII models. However, they almost went out of business many times.

In 1947, Aston Martin was bought by a tractor company

This was the start of Aston Martin's famous DB line of sports cars. The DB2 coupe was introduced at the New York Auto Show in 1950.

JAGUAR THROUGH THE YEARS

By the 1950s, people all over the world wanted to drive Jaguars! They started **exporting** cars to the United States.

In 1961, Jaguar introduced the E-Type at the Geneva Motor Show. Right away, it became known as one of the most beautiful sports cars of all time! The E-Type had a long, swooping hood and short, curved back. It was also fast and fun to drive without being too expensive.

This is a 1956 Jaguar XKSS. The XKSS is a D-Type racecar converted for road driving. Although many people wanted to own an XKSS, Jaguar made just 18 of these cars!

8TXK

Here, a number of Jaguar E-Types in different colors are on display at a vintage car show. More than 70,000 E-Types were sold between 1961 and 1974.

The Jaguar XJ-S luxury **grand tourer** followed the E-Type in 1975. The XJ-S had a more **aerodynamic** shape than the E-Type. It also came with a powerful V12 engine. Jaguar sold this car until 1996.

More About the E-Type

Today, the E-Type is considered an **icon** of 1960s design. A famous Italian car designer named Enzo Ferrari called the E-Type "the most beautiful car ever made." There is even a blue E-Type roadster in the Museum of Modern Art in New York City. Just five other cars are in the museum's collection with the E-Type!

ASTON MARTIN OVER TIME

Aston Martin introduced the DB4 sports car in 1958. The DB4's body was designed by an Italian company called Carrozzeria Touring. Carrozzeria Touring was famous for building super light cars with exciting shapes.

Aston Martin's next car was the DB5 luxury grand tourer in 1963. Many people thought it was one of the most beautiful cars ever made. The DB5 was also fast and powerful. It had

A 1935 Aston Martin Mark II racecar (car 67, in red) takes part in the 2012 Mille Miglia race. In this race, only cars built before 1957 can compete!

1952 Aston Martin DB3

a 4-liter 6-cylinder engine and a 5-speed manual transmission.

In 1964, the DB5 appeared in the James Bond movie *Goldfinger*. Right away, people wanted to own the car James Bond drove! This made Aston Martin very famous.

Aston Martin One-77

*Aston Martin's most famous limited edition car is the 2009 One-77. Just 77 were made. Each One-77 cost $1.4 million. This was Aston Martin's fastest, most powerful car of all time! The One-77 was built with a 6-liter V12 engine that could make 700 **horsepower** (HP)! This supercar had a top speed of 220 miles per hour (354 km/h).*

JAGUAR IN RACING

Jaguar has a long racing history. However, Jaguar is most famous for its amazing racing wins in the 1950s. Over seven years, Jaguar racecars won the 24 Hours of Le Mans race five times!

The 24 Hours of Le Mans is an **endurance** race held each year near Le Mans, France. Jaguar had its first win at Le Mans in 1951 with a C-Type. The C-Type had a lightweight tube-shaped body, which

This is the 1983 Jaguar XJR-5 racecar, built with a V12 engine. This car was driven by the Group 44 Racing team in the IMSA Camel GTP championship.

made it very aerodynamic. Another C-Type won at Le Mans in 1953.

After the C-Type, Jaguar designed a new racecar called the D-Type. Its body was wider and flatter than the C-Type, with curved sides. This design made the D-Type even more aerodynamic than the C-Type! Jaguar D-Types won at Le Mans three years in a row, starting in 1955.

ASTON MARTIN IN RACING

Aston Martin's racing history goes back to 1922. This was the year Aston Martin built two cars to compete in the French Grand Prix. The Aston Martin racing team also broke ten world records in 1922. In 1932, an Aston Martin International racing model won the Biennial Cup at Le Mans.

Aston Martin started to build its series of DB racecars in the

The racing version of the Aston Martin DB9 is called the DBR9. This car is built with a 6-liter V12 engine. Its carbon fiber body panels make this car lighter than the DB9.

Here, an Aston Martin V8 Vantage GT2 competes in the 2011 Super GT International Series in Malaysia. This is a powerful racing version of the V8 Vantage.

1950s. The DB3 was the first DB car built just for racing. It was very fast, but did not have many wins. The DBR1 had an aerodynamic design that made driver named Stirling Moss won the 1959 24 Hours of Le Mans race with a DBR1. This was Aston Martin's first and only win at the 24 Hours of Le Mans.

GOING HEAD-TO-HEAD

In the 1950s, Jaguar and Aston Martin were racing rivals. The Jaguar C-Type and D-Type racecars won five times at the 24 Hours of Le Mans between 1951 and 1957. However, Aston Martin worked hard on designing a racecar that could beat Jaguar. The DBR1 did just that in 1959.

Since the 1950s, neither Aston Martin nor Jaguar has had many racing wins. However, Jaguar has won the

1956 Jaguar D-Type

RRU 1

24 Hours of Le Mans two more times. A driver won in 1988 with a Jaguar XJR-9LM racecar. Another won with a Jaguar XJR-12 in 1990. Overall, Jaguar has had many more Le Mans wins than Aston Martin.

Comparing Performances

Car magazines and blogs often compare the performances of similar car models. This is another place you might see Jaguar and Aston Martin go head-to-head! For example, you might see a 2014 Jaguar F-Type V8 S compared with a 2014 Aston Martin V8 Vantage roadster. They have similar top speeds, but the Jaguar is much cheaper!

JAGUAR TODAY AND TOMORROW

Today, Jaguar makes both super cool luxury **sedans** and sports cars. Models in the XF line are smaller, sporty sedans. XJ models are full-size luxury sedans. The XK line includes Jaguar's two-door grand tourers. Jaguar also makes high-performance versions of each model.

In 2013, Jaguar introduced the super fast F-Type sports car. The 2014 F-Type V8 S is built with a 5-liter V8

This is the Jaguar C-X75 **concept car**. This car was introduced at the 2010 Paris Motor show. The X in its name stands for "experimental."

Jaguar S-Type

supercharged engine that can make 495 HP. This roadster can go from 0 to 60 miles per hour (0–97 km/h) in just 4.2 seconds! Jaguar's future may involve using **hybrid technologies**. Right now, Jaguar is working on concepts for a hybrid sports car!

Hybrid Concept Cars

Recently, Jaguar has designed concept cars that use hybrid technologies. The 2010 C-X75 was a concept for a plug-in supercar that could make 778 HP. The 2011 C-X16 was a concept for a hybrid electric sports car with a top speed of 186 miles per hour (299 km/h). In the future, we will see Jaguar experimenting with more hybrid technologies!

25

THE FUTURE FOR ASTON MARTIN

Today, Aston Martin has several different ranges of sports cars and sedans. The Vantage range includes coupes and roadsters built with V8 or V12 engines.

The DB9 is the latest model in Aston Martin's famous DB line. The 2014 Vanquish is the best performing Aston Martin of all time! This grand tourer can go from 0 to 60 miles

This is an Aston Martin Cygnet. This small 3-door hatchback car has low fuel emissions, making it very environmentally friendly. Drivers can squeeze this car into tiny parking spaces, too!

This is a racing version of the Aston Martin V12 Zagato. The V12 Zagato was built for the 50th anniversary of the super rare 1960 Aston Martin DB4 GT Zagato.

per hour (0–97 km/h) in just 4.2 seconds. The V12 Zagato is a superfast grand tourer that has competed in the 24 Hours of Nürburgring endurance race.

In the future, Aston Martin hopes to keep designing cool sports cars! Their focus is improving overall performance.

CC100 Concept Car

In 2013, Aston Martin introduced the CC100 concept car. The CC100 is a two-seat speedster, or superfast roadster, with a futuristic design. This car was built with a 6-liter V12 engine. The CC100 was made to celebrate Aston Martin's 100th anniversary. It is supposed to show the future direction of Aston Martin's car designs.

COMPARING CARS

Jaguar and Aston Martin are in a battle to be known as the best British sports car. Jaguar cars are less expensive than most Aston

Date Founded	**1922 (as Swallow Sidecar Company)**
Founders	**William Lyons and William Walmsley**
First Model	**1935 SS Jaguar 2.5 Litre Saloon**
Headquarters	**Whitley, Coventry, England**
Current Base Models in 2013–2014	**XF** **XJ** **XK** **F–Type**
Most Expensive Base Price, 2014	**2014 XKR-S GT** **$174,000**
Best 0–60 (0–97 km/h)	**2014 XKR-S GT** **3.9 seconds**
Top Speed	**1991 XJ220** **220 miles per hour (354 km/h)**
Most Powerful Engine	**2014 XKR-S/XKR-S GT** **5-liter supercharged V8, 550 HP**

Martins, making them more affordable. However, Aston Martin is seen as the more exclusive brand. Comparing these two British brands side-by-side can help you choose your favorite!

ASTON MARTIN

Date Founded	1913
Founders	Lionel Martin and Robert Bamford
First Model	1914 Aston Martin Coal Scuttle
Headquarters	Gaydon, Warwickshire, England
Current Base Models in 2013–2014	Vantage DB9 Rapide S Vanquish Zagato Cygnet
Most Expensive Base Price, 2014	2014 Vanquish $278,295
Best 0–60 (0–97 km/h)	2009 One-77 3.7 seconds
Top Speed	2009 One-77 220 miles per hour (354 km/h)
Most Powerful Engine	2009 One-77 6-liter V12 engine, 700 HP

YOU DECIDE!

Aston Martin and Jaguar both make cool British sports cars. They have been rivals for more than 75 years!

Aston Martins are more exclusive because they are much more expensive than Jaguars. Jaguar has had more racing successes than Aston Martin. Famous movie spy James Bond drives super sleek Aston Martins. The British Prime Minister rides around in a custom-built Jaguar.

Both brands have many fans around the world. Which is your favorite? Only you can decide!

Jaguar C-X75 Concept Car

Aston Martin DBS Carbon Edition II

GLOSSARY

aerodynamic (er-oh-dy-NA-mik) Made to move through the air easily.

concept car (KON-sept KAR) A car to show new features and technology.

endurance (en-DUR-ints) Strength and the ability to go long distances without getting tired easily.

exclusive (iks-KLOO-siv) Restricted in distribution, use, or appeal due to expense.

exporting (EK-spor-ting) Sending goods or services to another country for sale.

grand tourer (GRAHN TOOR-er) A luxury or performance car that is capable of long-distance driving or high speed.

horsepower (HORS-pow-er) The way an engine's power is measured. One horsepower is the power to lift 550 pounds (250 kg) 1 foot (.3 m) in 1 second.

hybrid technologies (HY-brud tek-NAH-luh-jeez) Technology that combines two or more distinct power sources to move a car.

icon (EYE-kon) A person or thing regarded as a symbol of something.

limited edition (LIH-muh-tid uh-DIH-shun) Limited to a specific number.

luxury (LUK-shuh-ree) Comforts and beauties of life that are not necessary.

production (pruh-DUK-shun) The method of making things.

rivals (RY-vulz) People or companies who try to beat others at something.

sedans (suh-DANZ) Cars that seat four or more people.

FURTHER READING

Hill, Randal C. *Aston Martin*. Fast Cars. Mankato, MN: Capstone Press, 2008.

Mezzanotte, Jim. *The Story of Jaguar*. Classic Cars. New York: Gareth Stevens, 2005.

Quinlan, Julia J. *Aston Martin*. Speed Machines. New York: PowerKids Press, 2013.

INDEX

For web resources related to the subject of this book, go to:
www.windmillbooks.com/weblinks
and select this book's title.

TABLE OF CONTENTS

BATTLE OF THE BRITS

If British sports cars are known for one thing, it is being super cool! For example, James Bond, the coolest spy in movie history, is famous for driving slick British sports cars. Two British carmakers in particular are known for making cool sports cars. These companies are Jaguar and Aston Martin.

Aston Martin and Jaguar have been **rivals** for more than 75 years. Both

> 2014 Jaguar
> F-Type